PRAISE F

"Mary's poems trea
ones I thought I had forgotten until I read *Lullaby for Mothers*. She has
this way of voicing the moments in between the big things, the ones
that are easy to miss yet carry the very signature of our mothering."
~ *TraceyKay Coe*

"In a world overflowing with books on how to parent my children,
Mary's wise words remind me that it is perhaps even more important
to relax enough to let them parent me. Her words have changed the
relationship I have with my children, myself, and my own mother, in
the most beautiful way." ~ *Annie Ferguson Muscato*

"I love Mary's poems – I re-read them often. We've never met, yet
she speaks for me as though she knows me and my life. I sometimes
wonder if Mary has snuck into my soul and stolen her words from
me."~ *Melissa Joseph Thorn*

"Mary's words are like silken threads that connect me to the vast
holiness of mothering – first through her experience, then my
own, then back through the fibres of my lineage. Her collection of
thoughts is timeless, giving me a solid place to stand as I continue to
explore my own identity as a mother." ~ *Michelle Wells, Creation Co-op*

"Mary has a way of quickly transporting her reader right into her
worlds, inner and outer, through her vivid and touching poetry.
The gentleness and honour she conveys on her experiences comes
through and touches the heart." ~ *Lauren Oujiri*

"Mary's craft distills intimate moments into nectar. We drink in
themes of innocence, protection, belonging, and trust. But above all,
we open to a lullaby of unbounded love." ~ *Cynthia Rome*

"Mary's poetry is breathtakingly beautiful." ~ *Jean Bonnitcha*

Published in New Zealand by
Castle Press
PO Box 47165
Upper Hutt 5143
New Zealand

First published in New Zealand 2019

A catalogue record is available at the National Library of New Zealand.

ISBN: 9781697248616 (paperback)
ISBN: 978-0-473-47612-0 (epub)

Cover design: Sara Gaspar
Cover illustration: Mirjam Siim
Typesetting: Sophie White

Printed by Kindle Direct Publishing

Lullaby for Mothers

motherhood, in poems

MARY WALKER

For my children

FOREWORD

In a world where children have often been seen as 'lesser' than adults, and where parenting hasn't been valued, parenting has often seemed to be a place simply of hard work and meaningless monotony. Yet we are seeing a revolution in the way we perceive children, and the way we value parenting.

In my work, I am passionate about helping parents see the tremendous gift of parenting: to help us become more present and compassionate; to help our children stay present and compassionate; and to help us value our children, ourselves, and our parenting journey.

In my own experience as a mother and Mothering Mentor, I have seen huge changes over the past seventeen years in the way children are treated and parenting is perceived.

I believe that parenting can be the most profound of experiences, where we wake dormant places in ourselves, heal old hurts, and find love and compassion that had long been buried. All so that we can help our children know they are unconditionally loved and valued— and find unconditional love for ourselves as we gradually get free from cultural constraints of punishment, judgment, coercion, shame and guilt.

I am passionate about inviting mothers to remember deep compassion for themselves rather than tread the old cultural path of guilt and comparison.

For me, poetry speaks to the ineffable wonder of parenthood and childhood. The moments of beauty in amongst the third load of washing or the caring for a sick child. The inherent transience of the experiences as our children constantly grow and become.

I love Mary's poetry. And I particularly love this collection of poems.

For me, they remind me of those deep soulful moments when we look into our child's eyes and everything else disappears, or we see the wonder of being alive through watching their experience of being alive and seeing the world through fresh eyes.

She helps us see the magic that lies behind the routine and repetition. The divinity in the everydayness. And most of all, the profound journey of deepening into ourselves and our hearts that mothering invites us to.

I wish all mothers could read this beautiful, soulful, magical book of poems.

Having them on your table or countertop, and reading one in the midst of a busy day might just transform how you experience what comes next.

Marion Rose Ph.D.
www.marionrose.net

INTRODUCTION

Everything is amplified when you're a mother—the depth of our love, the lengths we'll go to, the intensity of our fears and frustrations. The enormity of it can come upon us suddenly. Love itself can rush from the sky, pack itself densely into a single, ordinary moment, leaving us breathless.

Every worry about our children's future, or fear that we are letting them down, is a chance to soften, unravel and gently knit ourselves back together. Every difficult passage we navigate brings us closer to them, and returns us to ourselves. In those moments as a parent when we don't know what to do, we can return to what we feel. We can look for the moments when love was present and unshakeable.

Many poems in this book are ordinary moments with my children. They are specific to me but, I hope, speak to the universal experience of being a mother.

It is through the ordinary that we come to know our children. A moment that might look insignificant to someone else etches itself in our memory for life. It forges and strengthens us. It binds us to them, and them to us, over and over again.

In the end, motherhood is not a series of grand gestures, just as childhood is not a series of milestones. It is a mix of daily ministrations and bearing witness to a life unfolding. It is both mundane and sublime.

I hope these poems help you see your own moments.

CONTENTS

PART I   13

Unmapped   15

Limbs   16

Fingerprints   17

Marvellous   18

No Room   20

Dandelion   22

Creak   23

What You See   24

Fantail   25

Funeral for a Songbird   26

Painting Faces   28

Light   30

The Lesson   31

Lunch with My Father   32

Ferdinand   33

Bare Legs   35

Uncertainty   36

Life Is Not a Competition   37

Night Owl   38

Wild Fruit   39

I Offer You the Moon   40

Courage   41

PART II   43

Rain   44

Fever   45

Perspective   46

I, River   47

Guardian   48

Weather   49

Tectonic   50

Tend   51

It's Not Too Late   52

Home   54

Calling Out   55

Write Your Own Poem   57

Notes & Memories   59

PART I

UNMAPPED

Your surface gives no hint of you,
mere footprints in dust;
yet inside, you are a world,
unseeable landscape of crevice and fissure,
a place to go by feel.

A plink in the well echoes through you,
through veins of quartz and gold,
ringing off walls inscribed with light.

Above ground you stop,
looking for the source of your sound,
unaware you are cavernous,
canyon, cathedral—
turned inside out, stars navigate
by your light, skies weep.

LIMBS

Afraid of the dark, they find their way
to my bed at night; one hot, one cold
and no rest for any of us.

Sleepless elbows and knees find my hip,
shin, and the tender bone under my eye,
my body remembering a knot of child
kneading my bladder, stealing my breath,
stamping footprints on my belly.

These growing limbs—
needing new shoes, longer pants, another haircut;
these limbs that cling to me like vines to the face of a house—
they are working themselves free.

Against the curtain of their still small breaths,
truth dawns—these limbs will outlast me.
Worse, first
they will stop walking themselves
to my bedside at night.

FINGERPRINTS

Their traces are on every pane; I can chart their growth by the
glass I can still see through. Soft damp hands, jammy fingers,

a forehead or nose if the hands are full—they don't care
for cleaning them, and why should they?

What need do pirates, explorers and cave bears have
for vinegar and a lint-free cloth? Instead, we look at the world

through creased palms, smudges from the tips of splayed
fingers, like an x-ray of our days, a blueprint, a map.

Life is a breathless rush—moments too full, too busy
to turn handles, too much to lose by waiting

and wiping hands before throwing open windows and
bursting through doors. The day beckons.

Outside, the glass shows only reflections—trees, sky, and
laughing, moving bodies. I long to join them,

leave the proof of our well-lived lives where it is.
The last whorl will be wiped clean soon enough.

MARVELLOUS

I see her skeleton, sleeping;
mandible, cheekbone, cranium,
clavicle. The curve of her spine,
a question.

I made those bones
even the ones I cannot name.
This bed is a womb and
I am with her,
our two curled bodies asking
and asking the questions.

I feel every bone, the skin
of my face giving way to my
nose, pulled tight across my forehead
like a drum. Each hair as wide as
an oak. I am land. Blood gushes
through me, rivers run through me.

She'll be land one day too.
A three million year old fossil, a Lucy.
When she wakes, I'll teach her the song
Dry Bones. We'll learn the names
of the ones we do not know.
Where Lucy was found
in Ethiopia, they call her Dinkinesh—
they call her *you are marvellous*.

All these questions without answers,
yet still we ask and carry on
inhabiting our skeletons,
as if we chose to be here,
as if we really are.

NO ROOM

Question one, "what's that?"
I'd wondered how long it would take,
how long until they asked about the 10-foot fence
with its barbed wire top; how many rides past the
prison; how many times singing wheels-on-the-bus.

Question two, "what's a prison?"
I should have been prepared for,
with all that time waiting for the first.
Instead I stumbled, chains on my words.
Prison is heart-breaking to explain.

Question three, "a cage for people?"
Not so much a question, as a sentence—
to which the only answer is
yes.

Question four, "will I ever go to prison?"
The answer satisfied no one: choices, and
how you believe you have none, or truly
have none; a mumbling about futility and
fear, privilege, race, poverty, systemic failure,
revenge and sadness. Deep, deep sadness.

No answer at all to the thin line between thoughts
and acts; the way we sentence ourselves with
talk of good and bad; how we divorce ourselves
from our humanness when we pretend we haven't built
a ten-foot testament to fear.

No answer that avoids the implication
be good, or else.

No more questions.
There was no room in the car, no room
for anything else.

DANDELION

Save all of nature, she whispers before she blows
the dandelion clock. We watch the seeds in silence
because if someone hears your wish it won't come true.

Chainsaws whine on the hill across the valley.
That's a lot of insects without homes, she says,
so I reply with tree farms and replanting
but I can see what she is thinking: *tell that to the insects.*

We hear the cry of splintering wood, the rush of displaced air;
imagine, terribly, the sound of small things falling.
The arms of the dandelion float, pilots
looking to land, for a bare patch to signal them in.

Come spring there'll be a forest here, a jungle of dandelions,
hundreds of crayoned suns drawing butterflies, bees and moths.
One small wish, and a hundred yellow door mats
roll out, welcome.

CREAK

That, I say
is the timber talking,
rubbing shoulders,
telling stories
about the times
they used to creak
in the forest,
speaking green,
speaking sap,
languaging
whatever it is
trees language—
what they'll be
when they grow up, maybe,
and whether they'll be around
to see the kids grow—
knowing, at least,
wherever they go,
they'll always
still
have
language.

WHAT YOU SEE

I don't see what you see,
can't know the smell of a crowd,
the volume of your taste,
the colour of the words you ask me not to say.
I might assure you of safety,
exalt your efforts, urge you try again,
but you don't see what I see

and what a bird sees
is not what a hedgehog hears
or how a worm knows the rain.
I don't see what you see
but I search for windows all the same—
the things that crease your brow
or drain the colour from your face—
but you owe no explanation.

I won't ask for a window if there is none.
I won't ask you to puncture the wall,
fashion a frame, scoop the sand you hate to touch,
stand in the heat to make the glass
I won't ask you to smelt your precious energy—
not for me.

I don't need to see what the bird sees
to marvel at its flight,
wouldn't urge the hedgehog to look harder,
I would never doubt the wisdom of the worm.
Whatever you see, I see you,
and will guard your right to be.

FANTAIL

A fantail flutters at the window,
playing peekaboo with my children,
playing with the idea of coming inside
which means
somebody will die,
that's what people say.
And though I love to pass on stories to my children,
I will not pass on this.
I tell them a new story
about fantails being curious,
how they come to say hello,
and take home stories for their children.

I share the one the fantails tell—
about two-legged creatures who
live in boxes
and flap around when fantails visit;
how they want something to blame
when people die,
how they need to find a reason
when their people die—
look how they tell stories,
and look how they live
in boxes.

FUNERAL FOR A SONGBIRD

We conducted a funeral this morning. In gumboots and coat, in the soft grey fog, my five-year-old laid a songbird to rest at the foot of a gingko tree.

I found the bird on the laundry floor, taking it to the bin when my daughter walked in – feathers everywhere, the bird in my hand, and a teaspoon of blood between us.

She had seen dead birds before, but not like this. The bird still warm, the cat crouched in the corner. Life, and the end of it, hung in the air.

Her beloved had killed the bird and she held the confusion, found space to love the cat and mourn the bird. The bird's death was beautiful and sad. She did not shy from any part of it. My avoidance of grief looked childish.

My daughter chose the tree. "Because the bird might look up at the golden leaves and think they are its wings. And because the tree will drink the bird and become stronger."

The bird lay in its grave, ready to be covered. She climbed the tall, rickety ladder that leans against the gingko—the ladder she climbs when she wants to feel strong—and stood there a moment. Later, she told me "I climbed in case the bird looked up and thought I was flying".

The bird tucked safely in the earth, we walked back to the house. "Does the whole garden seem sad to you?"

She found a dewy spiderweb strung across the box hedge.
"The plant asked the spider to do that so it would be beautiful for the bird."

"Those branches are hanging low because they feel so sad."

"That tree lost its leaves because it cried them all off."

Finally, at the back door, "it was only one bird," and she smiled. "There are lots more."

One bird may be dead, but the garden has never been so alive.

PAINTING FACES

She longs to be a cat
and last night lapped milk
from a blue china bowl.
Paint my face, she asks
so today we paint her face,
patting it white
with pink for her nose
and the rose of her cheek
though the only true pink on a cat
is its tongue,
and that she has already.

Is this where it starts? The pretending?
No, this is not like her
hating her chocolatey hair—
wishing it longer, prettier, golden.
Is six too young for that?
It seems too young for that.
I freckle the curve of her smile with black,
it tickles, she giggles,
I smudge it, and sigh.

Sorry, she says
as I whisker her face
with a flick of the wrist,
like the lines she'll paint under her eyes
one day.
She is still now—
Like a cat in the sun,
breath warm and milky.
I look for the parts of her that can't be painted over
as she searches my face.
I love you, she whispers
barely moving.

LIGHT

We pull the blanket over our heads and shield our closed eyes.
Nose to nose we dive in the dark

waiting for our pupils to open. When we feel the black tide
pulling, opening, like owls observing

the night, we fling back the covers, spring open our eyes,
and watch the black pools shrink.

Your wide eyes and small hands hold my face; the power
enchants you. We pitched a sun

into the night, alarmed the owl, dried up the lakes. There's only
so much of your light I can take

but I laugh and do it over. Outside on the blackening pond,
lilies close their petalled lashes.

THE LESSON

In the swimming pool
she asks for the platform to be moved;
for the teacher to push it deeper, further out.
Her arms, legs, the turning of her head,
once strange pieces of a broken clock,
are coming into line.
She feels the pull for space.

This is how things come together,
falling into place like a penny in a slot,
the last click in the sequence of a combination lock.
It cannot be forced or taught, only felt.
Invisible pieces align; we coalesce—
we pull ourselves through life's blue water
and find we can breathe freely.

LUNCH WITH MY FATHER

The soft-boiled egg
takes him back to his father's knee,
to an egg held in a piece of cloth,
to a working man's lunch;
back to crowding 'round for the top of the egg,
a mouthful in a small white bowl.
My daughter wants the
egg for its runny yellow yolk,
to give thin white soldiers
golden boots which she'll eat, and leave the rest.
I wince at the waste
in the wake of his story. But he's smiling
at the memory of his da, and smiling
at the smile on his granddaughter's face,
and I wonder at the luck of time and place,
at the hairline crack
that makes an egg a spoonful of riches
on one side,
paint for a canvas, the other.

FERDINAND

Like a mouse
watching bulls, battling
is how he says he feels, playing
with his friends.

Years ago
we met Ferdinand the bull
resting against a tree—
he had a favorite spot out in the pasture under
a cork tree...he would sit in its shade all day.
He pointed and said, that's me
that's me at school.

They ask
why don't you run and play with all the other
little bulls and skip and butt your head
I guess, because bulls are made for fighting
and children are for play.

I like it better here,
where I can sit just quietly.

His mother saw that he was not lonesome.
It's okay to sit under a tree, I said, to play
in different ways.

Except he is
                    lonesome.

I want to reread the book.
I want to ask Ferdinand
how are you now?
Were the cork trees enough? The butterflies
and the flowers, were they company?
Is it true you were not lonesome?

He must be very old.
His mother will be gone. I want to know,
I want to ask
did you find someone else to understand?

Extracts from *Ferdinand The Bull*, by Munro Leaf.

BARE LEGS

Whenever Mum couldn't find him,
to the plum tree she'd send me,
knowing I'd see my brother's bare legs
hanging down, kicking,
him sat wedged in the crook of the tree,
chest hidden by leaf and ruby plum,
stones falling like missiles on the ground beneath him.

Now whenever I can't find him,
to the grape house I go,
knowing I'll see my son's bare legs
on the pitted wooden stool,
chest hidden by leaf and purpled bunches,
eating straight from the vine,
stripped stems littering the ground beneath him.

UNCERTAINTY

In a rare moment alone in the car, he says
"there's nothing certain in life, is there?"

In front the narrow road unwinds, waves
slap the sea wall and I have to say, no

not much is certain, but some things are, like
I will love you, always.

On a tight bend between ocean and cliff,
salt blinding the windscreen, he says

"like, it's not certain our car will stay on the road."
Probability, save me here.

I'm driving carefully and I'm paying attention
and it's likely we'll stay on the road, but no

nothing is certain.

I ease off the pedal, the wipers work at the ocean's tears,
and my son stares out at all the things he cannot know.

How to answer a child who has the perilous world in his sights,
except with yes, and I will love you, always.

LIFE IS NOT A COMPETITION

Life is not a competition, began the story I wrote
for my son. One to make sense of the world.

"Is everything in life a competition?" he had asked.
I wondered why he thought that. But then—why would he not?
Pass the parcel, pin-the-tail, running race, talent show,
cooking contest, football matches, lottery, raffle,
top of the class, finals, the best schools, report cards,
top tier, ivy league, performance reviews, promotions,
best-dressed, the rich list, the oscars, the grammies,
pullitzer, booker, the cover of time,
even peace is a noble prize.

Social stories are for people for whom
the world does not make sense.
They don't see it quite right, you see?
All those things don't mean what they seem to
apparently.

Yes, people are competing for resource, position,
job, money, status, prize, accolade, reward,
while most everyone else fights to stay alive
or are too tired to fight, or
are just plain busy dying
but, no, as the story goes,
life is not a competition.

NIGHT OWL

The owl would cry outside
and he'd run to our bed at night.
So as not to fear the talons,
blood moon eyes, efficient beak;
so as not to—let's be honest—
disrupt our precious sleep,
we said Old Ruru lives way off,
two creeks, two farms, five hedges away
in the tree by the one-way bridge.

It's just his voice that travels, see?
It's just his call you hear,
like a lighthouse flashing—
here I am
here I am
and who
who is out there?

Now questions scratch his window at night—
what's my purpose,
why am I here—
as if Old Ruru left them
on the sill like prey or prayer,
these questions we cannot answer
from places we cannot see,
from our stuttering hearts,
from our one-way bridge,
as we cling to the dark
in our tree.

WILD FRUIT

Beyond my garden fence
weeds are simply plants.
I might rip blackberry from my borders,
but I covet its fruit in the wild.

You may not fit where you are;
too big for small spaces
too loose for tight boundaries
too loud, too colourful
too new.

Over the fence
the world is hungry for you;
you belong, out there.
Arch your canes over the gate,
beg the birds to lift you.
However you do it,
go free.

I OFFER YOU THE MOON

The telescope stands in the dark.
A flat moon rises above the poplars.
Put a coat on, I say. It's cold out.

We feel our way along the house,
down shadowed steps to where
the telescope stands waiting.

Careful not to bump it,
turn these knobs to focus,
look through the eyepiece, here.

I take a step back.
Good god, my father says.
Oh my god, says my mother. *Oh my god.*

Then, what everyone does:
stand back, look for the moon in the sky,
wonder—can they be the same thing? *God.*

Trace craters, strings of mountain beads, smudged
grey seas, continents; feel the urge to reach out a hand,
I could touch the moon.

My mother breathes *thank you.*
They are delighted, like children,
like it was me who offered them the world.

COURAGE

Courage
to step off the road,
to walk no path
when your child needs to go somewhere
the road does not.

Courage
to take your child by the hand
and walk away
knowing all that is given up,
all that may be lost.

Courage,
when you drag your eyes from the road at last
to find your child already gone—
waist high in meadow, approaching
a creek, a hawk freewheeling above.

PART II

RAIN

I know you're tired,
lurching from one exhausted moment
to the next,
rushed through life
like a cloud
at the mercy of the wind.

It's a relief, isn't it,
to let go, let out
what weighs heavy on your heart;
to lie on the shoulder of the hill
and weep.

You're not asked to hold it all.
Life invites release,
places mountains in your path
to clear the skies
and water
all that you watch over.

What the cloud never sees
is that the valley floor
blooms
after rain.

FEVER

Long before
the autumn rains,
the settled dew greens
the land's grazed face.

Mother
lifts our fevered head,
offering one small spoon
at a time.

It is the air itself
that saves us.
Night's cool cover, a cloth
on our burning face.

We long for a downpour,
forgetting
we need only a little, often.

One teaspoon of mercy,
one well-timed act of grace.

PERSPECTIVE

At the foot of a sprawling sky,
before the wide arms of the ocean,
I hear my name,
earth's curve whispering to me
    feel small,
        be awed.

Through my car window, the back door,
over the top of my children's heads
it crooks its finger at me—
    come, look out,
        look up.

The sky may dwarf me
but it invites me still;
the unreachable horizon
lets me play in its waters.

And when I dare,
when small and awed is no longer enough,
something new:

from somewhere, I am the horizon,
from out there, I'm part of the sky.

I, RIVER

Every river has its life.
The young, sinuous
carving and sculpting rocks,
rushing forward in waterfalls,
haste, haste
grit and hurry.

It is not will
that carries me now, but trust
and the ocean's deep call.
In the opening out of a life
time expands and lands unfold,
bowing, allowing me through.

I lay back and trust.
Like water, I find my own level.
Cupped in earth's hands,
I cover fathoms
with no effort at all.
Watch now as I braid this land.
Listen, I sing of the sea.

GUARDIAN

The idea is appealing.
With one clean cut
you could rise up in a new life.
It's tempting to
slice through
the undergrowth,
concrete the marsh,
level your uneven.

Hold on.
This is not just swamp you tread—
this is fallen forest,
rich with the seeds of your life to come.
Let it emerge softly.
Look for an opening—
a gap between trees,
where the light falls, playing,
inviting you in.

Put down the scythe—
go gently, let the clearing appear.
Love yourself as land,
see how you grow.

WEATHER

It's easy to love life under blue skies,
arms thrown wide to the weather,
sun shining, highlighting
life's soft curves.

Who are you when the clouds come?
Who are you in the rain?
Where does loss hide,
where does the hurt pool,
unable to find its way home?

The earth may take the rain in time,
and storms are only passing through.
Still, things can be done—
pain unearthed,
your life, aerated,
wounds and aches
brought home to light.

Land has its natural balance
and you have yours.
A loving state,
able to welcome the rain.

TECTONIC

You could say we are adrift,
but only if we were separate.
You could fear the random ruptures
or see the land answering its own call.
The solid ground you walk on rides a mantle
moved by its own shapeless heat.
There is fire in the belly.

You boil with an urge to express
and a heat that cares nothing
for your tidy arrangements.
Land reinvents itself, rising up,
creating new places to stand,
taking down the old—
the known sacrificed for the new, again and again.

Secure your life as much as you like.
Take a snapshot.
Today's landscape is no match for your burning core.
Your past is no match for the mountain.

TEND

I gather fallen limbs,
handle brittle lichened bones
with reverence,
returning them
to the base of their tree.
It is a privilege to warm the cloth,
to clean the hands of a child,
wipe the face of a loved one
who can no longer.
I tend to the dying tree
knowing one day
this will be me.
When I cannot
hold the spoon to my own mouth,
when the soup spills,
when I am spilling over
and my body no longer
contains me
may someone hold me,
hold the cup to my lips,
hold the paper to my pen,
hold me while I fall.

IT'S NOT TOO LATE

to build rock walls with your bare hands,
to lay brick paths,
weave a nest,
make sculpture for your garden.

There's still time
to draw and paint,
to make real
the pictures in your mind, and
birth the lands you visit
when you dream.

It's not too late
to go to wild places,
alone,
and unafraid.
Stand on the cliff tops,
stare at the heaving sea,
drape yourself
like weed over its rocks.

You could still remember how to roar,
make your body strong,
feel like you belong in it.

It's not too late to write
all the things that whisper to you.
Press your ear to the chest of the earth
and hear its quiet breathing.
Trace a vein,
listen for that which has no name yet.
Name it.

You could change gear,
go slowly.
Move through the world
through each day
at your own pace;
drop to the grass,
follow the ant's path
through the forest
if you choose.

Disregard the rules.
Drop them like a heavy coat.
Follow the call,
sure as an ancient traveller following stars
as they sail the blind ocean.
Set out, sail free.
Navigate by the star that you are.

HOME

On the day you finally meet yourself
like a weary traveller home
you will know it;
the way a child knows her mother's hand,
as something felt,
remembered.
You will know it in your flesh,
in the softening of your gait,
in the moment that you finally
finally
slip off your shoes
and allow yourself
to rest.

CALLING OUT

You think there's time. All the time in the world to share what you
think they need to know.

But you know you'll be chasing them down in the end,
as if they've forgotten their lunch, calling out the things
you missed along the way—assume the best in people;
be gentle with yourself; change your toothbrush regularly;
pay attention to each moment—to the way your hands
move as they wash the evening dishes, the way they move
like otters, like your hands were born to water.

It'll be too late by then. They'll be out of earshot, too far
off, too many concentric circles out of range. You'll be left
hoping you did enough. You'll hope they'll be okay,
And that you taught them well.

But then, maybe the wind shifts, just so. Maybe their pace
slows, their body turns back toward you slightly, head tilted
a fraction, listening. Maybe you get one last chance—

      forget everything else I said.
               just, I love you.

WRITE YOUR OWN POEM

Would you like to write your own poem
celebrating a moment with your child?

Access Mary's free online course at
www.marywalker.co.nz

Email: **mary@marywalker.co.nz**

Instagram: **@mary_walker_writer**

Facebook: **Mary Walker**

NOTES & MEMORIES

NOTES & MEMORIES

NOTES & MEMORIES

NOTES & MEMORIES

NOTES & MEMORIES

Made in United States
North Haven, CT
13 May 2023

36521585R10039